THE GHOSTLY TALES OF TOLEDO

Published by Arcadia Children's Books
A Division of Arcadia Publishing
Charleston, SC
www.arcadiapublishing.com

Copyright © 2024 by Arcadia Children's Books
All rights reserved

Spooky America is a trademark of Arcadia Publishing, Inc.

First published 2024
Manufactured in the United States

Designed by Jessica Nevins
Images used courtesy of Shutterstock.com; p. 2 T-I/Shutterstock.com.

ISBN: 978-1-4671-9759-5
Library of Congress Control Number: 2024939044

Notice: The information in this book is true and complete to the best of our knowledge. It is offered without guarantee on the part of the author or Arcadia Publishing. The author and Arcadia Publishing disclaim all liability in connection with the use of this book.

All rights reserved. No part of this book may be reproduced or transmitted in any form whatsoever without prior written permission from the publisher except in the case of brief quotations embodied in critical articles and reviews.

Spooky America

THE GHOSTLY TALES OF TOLEDO

BETH HESTER

Adapted from *Haunted Toledo* by Chris Bores

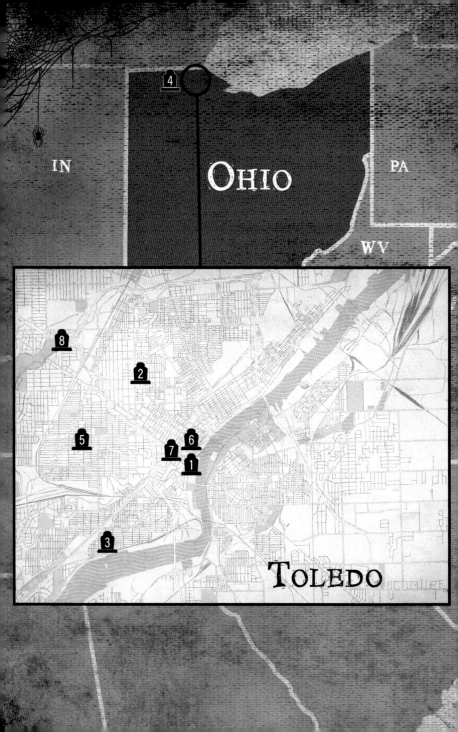

Table of Contents & Map Key

Welcome to Spooky Toledo!................... 3

1. Chapter 1. Oliver House 7
2. Chapter 2. Collingwood Arts Center.................. 19
   Chapter 3. Toledo Express Airport 33
3. Chapter 4. Games & Ghosts at the Waterfront............ 39
4. Chapter 5. Haunted Restaurants & Bars 53
   Chapter 6. A Book Break.......................... 73
5. Chapter 7. Spooky Schools 79
6. Chapter 8. Historic Downtown 85
7. Chapter 9. Repertoire Theatre 95
8. Chapter 10. Woodlawn Cemetery 99

A Ghostly Goodbye 105

Welcome to Spooky Toledo!

Imagine a city where glassmakers, sports teams, and awesome art all come together—that's Toledo, Ohio! The fourth largest city in Ohio (after Columbus, Cleveland, and Cincinnati), Toledo is a major trade center and busy Great Lakes port.

Toledo was founded in 1833 on the west bank of the Maumee River and was originally part of Monroe County, Michigan Territory.

After the Toledo War, it became part of Ohio in 1837. When the Miami and Erie Canal was finished in 1845, Toledo grew quickly. Its location on the railway line between New York City and Chicago also helped it grow. In the 1880s, the first glass manufacturers came to Toledo, earning it the nickname "The Glass City."

Today, Toledo is known for its vibrant arts community, car manufacturing, education, healthcare, and sports teams. But did you know that the Glass City is *also* known for its ghosts? From creaky old mansions with creepy shadows to dark basements that answer back, Toledo, Ohio, is full of haunted hot spots! Some are easy to find—like the beautiful old buildings of Collingwood Arts Center, which practically *shriek* "spooky." In other places, ghosts might be the last thing on your mind...but then suddenly they'll find *you*—with a tap on the shoulder while you're enjoying a plate of spaghetti, or watching a play, or choosing a book at the library.

In these pages, you'll get the inside story of some amazing paranormal locations and the spirits who haunt them—all researched by ghost hunter and Toledo local Chris Bores himself. Are you ready to meet the ghosts of Toledo? Let's go!

Oliver House

When planning Toledo's first high-class hotel, Major William Oliver chose a location on Broadway Street, close to the train station. That way, travelers arriving in the new city would see it right away... and Major Oliver wanted to make sure they were wowed from the start. From the outside, his new hotel would be a large, dramatic structure built to impress. Inside, guests would find top-quality finishes at every turn. William Oliver had big plans for the hotel that would bear his name.

All this attention to detail meant construction took seven whole years to complete—so long that Major Oliver died by the time it was done, leaving his daughter, Hattie, to take up management. Hattie and her husband, James, did not disappoint. They opened the hotel in 1859 to great fanfare. Visitors must have been amazed by the modern luxuries they met at every turn, such as running water, steam heaters, and even Toledo's first wallpaper. The furnishings were so cutting-edge that staff had to teach visitors how to use them without harming themselves. Guests unfamiliar with gaslights might have tried to blow them out like a candle—and start a gas leak that filled their rooms with deadly gas! If you could avoid the perils of the technology of the times, however, you'd find plenty to enjoy, including a billiard room, a barber shop, and a restaurant that could be used as a grand ballroom for parties.

How much would all this luxury cost? About two and a half dollars per night. It's a bargain compared to today's hotels, but it was a lot of money back then!

About forty-five years later, when demand at the hotel had increased (and wallpaper and plumbing weren't such big news anymore), new owners divided the hotel, renting out half of the building as warehouse space for other businesses. Eventually, however, even half of a hotel proved too costly to run in such a massive space. In 1919, the sixty-year-old building was sold, emptied of its fancy furnishings, and divided into a place where many businesses could find a home. It was similar to a shopping center with different vendors renting space, and a branch of the Ohio Savings Bank complete with two large bank vaults.

Over time, the building continued to change, never regaining its former glory. Never, that is, until the 1990s. That's when Jim and Patricia Appold bought the building and started restoring it. New apartments took shape on the guest floors, restaurants and meeting rooms were added downstairs, and some of the building's old glamour seemed to return. But according to builders and restaurant staff who worked at the refurbished Oliver House, glamorous architecture wasn't the only thing stirred up from the past.

One employee recalled, "That place is very haunted. I saw and heard things that could not be explained... several shadow figures... moaning and loud noises coming from the basement. Someone said there was a tunnel underneath." There are, in fact, tunnels under the building, which may once have led to the Maumee River. This may once have been an innocent way to bring supplies from the river to the hotel. It may also have been a way to get secrets out of the hotel—and keep crimes out of sight.

Bootleggers & Bodies

During the Prohibition Era, a time when drinking alcohol was illegal in the United States, it's said that "bootleggers" illegally sold alcohol out of the basement. Perhaps the Oliver House's tunnels were a pathway for shipments to reach boats on the river without being spotted by law enforcement.

Bootlegging was a dangerous business, after all. It was against the law, which means everyone involved was a criminal! They were willing to do anything to keep their secrets hidden and their competition out of the way. But could some of that dark, murderous energy still be lingering inside the Oliver House all these years later? Ghost hunter Chris Bores has studied a ghostly presence who may be linked to the tunnels. He's found an intriguing match to the story of a "murdered maid" from the old days of the Oliver Hotel.

As the story goes, a housekeeper began a secret romance with a rich patron, a man of unlimited means. But soon, the man grew anxious the relationship could damage his reputation.

His solution? *Murder.*

He hired two hitmen to kill his

former lover, roll her in a blanket, and drag her through the tunnels to the river.

There's another (legal) business now selling drinks on-site: a brewery where customers enjoy great food and local beers. Many diners don't even notice the ghostly presence lurking there...but some ghost hunters think this place is haunted by the murdered maid.

One psychic said she instantly felt a female presence from the early days of the hotel: "She was murdered and doesn't know what happened." Chris Bores thinks he found the same spirit in the banquet room, where his ghost-sensing device picked up these mysterious words: "highway" and "malicious."

Could this be the housekeeper trying to describe her murder and the tunnel "roads" used to dispose of her body? It might be...and she might just stick around until the mysteries of her death are brought to light.

Kidding Around

Most of the youthful spirits in the hotel are much happier—even playful. Of course, the end of their lives wasn't so happy. One boy, the son of a banker, was playing on the banister at the top of a tall, grand staircase when he fell to his death on the floor below. A little girl may have spent her living days here when the building was a "flophouse" during the Great Depression. When families had lost all their money, they found shelter in flophouses. These days, however, the Oliver House's "kid" ghosts seem to be all about fun! One little girl shows

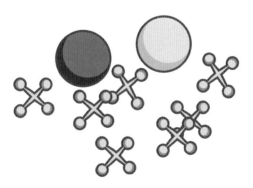

extra energy when a puppy comes to the hotel, and several of the children perk up when new ghost-hunting gadgets come to investigate.

You don't need pets or fancy equipment to have a ghostly encounter with these teasing tots, however: just take a stroll through the main banquet room or spend some time in Rockwell's Fireside Room. You might feel a tug on your clothes or a poke on your arm. You might see things moving around with nobody pushing them. You might even get a pinch on the butt! But don't worry—that's just the Oliver House kids welcoming you to their playground.

The Childless Mother

If you find the Oliver House children, you might also come across their caretaker, the widow of an 1890s soldier. She was a young bride when her husband left Toledo for the Spanish-American War,

and she was one of hundreds who attended a grand farewell party for the soldiers at Oliver House before the men shipped out.

The new wife eagerly awaited the return of her beloved—and the birth of their first child. Sadly, though, her husband never did return from war. In her heartache, the widow lost her

pregnancy, too. It is said that's why she cares for the ghostly children like a mother, sometimes preventing visitors from interacting with them. And the spirit children are not the only ones she tries to protect. When pregnant women come to Oliver House, they sometimes feel a gentle touch on their arm or a guiding push or pull near their feet. Perhaps it is the widow doing her best to protect these mothers-to-be.

Collingwood Arts Center

In the years after Major Oliver built his grand hotel, Toledo's population was growing, and the young city was thriving. A business-minded person could make a fortune selling everything Toledoans needed, like food, kitchenware, and hardware. That's what merchant Christian Gerber did, and it made him rich enough to build the three-story mansion of his dreams. Inside were fifteen-foot ceilings, the finest wood and furnishings, marble mantles over the many fireplaces, and a stunning front staircase.

There was only one problem—in the end, Gerber's tastes outran his budget. When his business slowed down, he had no choice but to sell his extravagant new home.

The Gerber House changed hands a couple of times, winding up in the hands of St. Ursula Academy. Under the careful management of the nuns, the home was renovated for use as a girls' school. The back of the house was replaced with a grand, domed auditorium with glittering chandeliers in the center. A balcony with private galleries, where the nuns could watch performances without being exposed to the public eye, was also added.

When the Academy wanted to build additional structures on the grounds, they joined forces with Mary Manse College to help pay for the construction. The campus grew by seven new buildings, including a gym, more classrooms, and a maintenance building. It was renamed Mary Manse College and St. Ursula Academy, and it was a success for decades. By the 1970s, however, the number of students dwindled. Mary Manse College officially closed in 1979, and everyone left the campus. At least, that was the plan. With the school officially vacant, waves of unofficial residents started moving through.

In the early 1980s, people used the vacant buildings to perform strange rituals. They would call upon dark energy and leave eerie graffiti everywhere. Squatters—people who live in a place without filing paperwork or paying rent—moved into the dorms. It didn't take long for the whole place to take on a run-down, forbidding feeling. Then a new day came for the site when the Collingwood Arts Center bought the property in 1985. The Arts Center's goal was to offer affordable housing for artists and a place to display and perform their art.

Soon the halls were filled with life again. Artists worked on their creations in studios. Hallways were lined with colorful paintings propped against the walls. But as the artists soon discovered, that wasn't the only thing in the halls of the old St. Ursula's and St. Mary Manse. An ominous presence seemed to lurk in some cold corners. Was it a dark shadow of

those occult rituals from the squatter days? Anything is possible, as you will soon read.

Balcony Breakfast Bunch

Most theaters have a balcony, but what was special about the balcony built for St. Ursula Academy was the sections reserved for the Ursuline nuns. The galleries were like little alcoves where the nuns could sit during performances. They could see the stage, but the public couldn't see them. It seems at least one of those nuns found this spot so comfortable, she doesn't want to leave. Some evenings, a shadow figure can be seen in an upper alcove at the back of the balcony.

Those solitary audience moments aren't the only times the nuns enjoyed the theater. It's said they also liked to gather for their morning coffee in the balcony. That might explain why people sometimes notice the smell of coffee and toast floating through the theater. (Quick question: Did you just make toast? Neither did we. Weird.)

That said, if you find yourself in the theater and catch the scent of coffee in the air, or if you spot a mysterious figure darting across the balcony, don't be afraid—it might just be an Ursuline nun getting ready for the day or hoping to catch the next school play. She probably thinks you can't see her up there, and that's just the way she likes it.

Prop Room

There's at least one other ghostly nun, though, who doesn't mind being known. A room on the fifth floor once served as a storage space for props and other supplies for theater performances. One day, a ten-year-old boy went up there to get a prop for the production. When he came back down, he told his mom he was surprised because he thought all the nuns had moved out of the building. She didn't know what to make of this. Of course all the nuns had moved out—they'd been gone for decades! There shouldn't have been anyone on the fifth floor—just props. The boy explained, "I was talking to a nun on the fifth floor who wanted to tell me how much she enjoyed seeing us children practicing for our play."

Collingwood Kids

A first-floor bathroom in the classroom wing is the haunt of Caroline, a student from the old days when the property was a school for girls. This teenage ghost is said to have a flair for the dramatic: she's caused the toilets to flush and faucets to turn on and off on their own. But Caroline's most dramatic move by far is her woeful wailing. Visitors have heard sorrowful sobbing coming from the empty bathroom. Some people, feeling sorry for the girl who seems so sad and alone, go inside to see if they can comfort whoever is inside. But as soon as they open the door, the crying stops...and all they find is an empty room!

Next to Caroline's bathroom, an old classroom rings with

the echoes of children's conversations at night... even though the room is empty. Could these late-night conversations be the cause of her sadness? No one knows.

There's another child-ghost at Collingwood who doesn't fit the typical mold of a St. Ursula student. In the third-wing basement, ghost-hunter Chris Bores encountered not a teenage girl, but a little boy. And this was no ordinary little boy: one day, Chris brought a bouncy ball down to the basement as an offering for the boy to play with. He asked the boy to move the ball, then turned away. Sure enough—when Chris turned back around, the ball had moved! "Not only that," said Chris, "but the ball was vibrating like crazy. The spirit had definitely disturbed it."

So, who was this little boy, and what was he doing in the girls' school? Chris did some research and discovered that a boy named Joey Harmon had been on the construction site while that section of the school was being built way back in 1905. Joey must have been a fearless kid—after all, he was the kind of ghost who would interact with ghost hunters and try to move physical objects. During life, he was the kind of kid who would climb onto a tall roof to play—which is exactly what he was doing when he fell to his death so long ago. Sad but true: being fearless is overrated—and deadly!

THE DARK PRESENCE

Many people have reported a feeling of darkness that takes no form at Collingwood. Witnesses find it tricky to describe but mostly agree: when this dark force enters a room, warmth and joy seem to exit. It could be left over from the days when people performed occult rituals here, but whatever it is, we recommend going the other way if you encounter it!

How will you know it's there? You'll suddenly feel uneasy, frightened, maybe even terrified. Your senses will notice a change in temperature as coldness descends and a shift in the light as darkness takes over. Deeper senses may pick up a shift in the room's energy. You might feel frozen in place—some people do. Don't panic: the freeze begins to thaw, eventually....

Guardian Angels

In this place that has been filled with caring nuns, children, and art, it's no surprise there are also helpful spirits. Some even heroically helpful—such as the aptly named Sister Angelique, who might be behind the astonishing story told by Patrick, a handyman at Collingwood.

Patrick was working in the theater on a tall ladder when he suddenly lost his balance. In an instant, he knew he was doomed. There was nothing within reach to grab, and he was far, far above the floor below. He would surely fall all the way down. But he reached out by reflex, and his hand grasped on to a perch, allowing him to climb to safety.

Patrick looked back at the scene and knew there was no way he could have reached that spot. It was ten feet from where he had fallen.

There was only one explanation that made sense to Patrick: someone had intervened and glided his body from one spot to another. It must have been one of the nuns or a guardian angel. Or simply one and the same.

Toledo Express Airport

These days, flying by airplane is one of the safest ways to travel. But when Toledo Express Airport opened in 1954, passenger air travel was still relatively new, and there were fewer safety regulations than there are now. From the time Toledo Express opened its runways, five airplanes have had fatal crashes at or near the airport. They have included a mail plane with a pilot and copilot, a DC-8 military cargo plane with four crew members aboard, a private jet on a training flight, and a cargo plane arriving from Texas.

The first of the five crashes, though, had the most fatalities: In 1960, a plane was carrying the California Polytechnic State University football team home from a game against Bowling Green State University, on a night with fog so thick you could barely see a thing. In those days, a pilot could make a

final decision whether to fly in such thick fog. In this case, it was most definitely the wrong decision. The plane rumbled along the runway with forty-eight people on board, including players, coaches, and managers. It crashed mere moments after liftoff, killing twenty-two of the people on board, including sixteen players.

New rules were put in place after that. Now, the air traffic controllers say when it's safe to take off, not the pilot. Still, more than thirty people have perished on these runways. It's no wonder Toledo Express Airport is said to be so haunted! The night crew at the airport reports the most supernatural activity, including the sound of footsteps on the stairs of the air traffic control tower and lights turning on and off by themselves. Could those pilots killed in crashes be trying to keep the air-traffic controllers alert? Maybe they want to prevent future accidents by making sure everyone is on their toes.

Some staffers have spotted the ghostly figure of a woman in the break room, and they've even smelled her perfume and heard her talking. Other sights and sounds are less specific: a shadow darting by, a feeling of being watched, and "odd" noises. It appears, at least, that most of the ghosts are content to be where they are. That's a good thing—if any of them are still waiting for a connecting flight, they might be out of luck!

Games & Ghosts at the Waterfront

Did you know there have been multiple amusement parks in Toledo? Two early favorites opened in 1895. There was Walbridge Park on the Maumee River, as well as the Casino and Scenic Railway Park on Lake Erie. Both proved popular with Toledoans, who could cool off at the waterfront on hot summer days. Both locations offered a wide range of attractions to keep them entertained.

Walbridge Park featured a pavilion, greenhouses, and beach at the beginning, and then grew into a fair, with bumper cars and a figure-eight wooden roller coaster by the 1920s. Another early feature was a woodchuck—donated in 1899 to launch a modest menagerie. By the end of that year, the number of animals in the Walbridge Park Zoo rose to thirty-nine.

The park continued to grow in size and fame over the next few decades, adding attractions all the while: a sea lion pool (1904); lions, elephants, and zebras (1911); and shelter houses and lakes (1930s). It was a favorite with locals, who could hop on a trolley from downtown to spend a day boating, taking a turn on the merry-go-round, and marveling at the exotic animals—all while enjoying the waterside breezes on a hot summer day.

At Scenic Railway Park, patrons could snack at concession stands, visit the bowling alley, or take aim in the shooting gallery on the beautiful coast of Lake Erie. To enjoy the cooling lake breezes and a better view of the boats from Toledo Yacht Club, people could take a leisurely stroll from the casino building

to a distance of 1,200 feet out over the lake on a wooden boardwalk—or zoom there on Toledo's first wooden roller coaster, which ran parallel to the pier. Thanks to the new trolley line, this mini-vacation was an easy day trip for Toledoans. Even better, the casino and yacht club joined forces to host showstopping events such as boxing matches, dances, and air shows. Together, they were a truly special destination.

However, Scenic Railway Park suffered a series of fires that led to its undoing. Tragically,

the final fire occurred during an event attended by hundreds. It was late June 1910, nearing midnight, when the partygoers noticed the flames. The crowd erupted into activity, everyone trying to flee at once, but the flames spread too quickly. In the panic, many were trampled. Others suffocated, unable to escape the building. Fatalities totaled 519 that fateful night. The carefree days of Scenic Railway Park were over.

Toledo Yacht Club, however, survived and thrived on the Lake Erie waterfront. Members and patrons might enjoy a day sailing on the lake, then come to the clubhouse to visit with friends or relax with a drink at the bar. Customers liked it so much, in fact, some of them have lingered on after closing time... WAY after closing time!

One bartender heard a man order a Manhattan cocktail, but when she turned around to confirm the order, he was gone! She's sure it was a former head of the yacht club—and other employees say they've heard the same invisible commodore.

If you find yourself on the first floor of the yacht club and get the strange feeling that you might have just seen something—even though there's nothing there—you could be right. And you wouldn't be the first one: shadow figures have been known to dart through those rooms. They may be connected to the disembodied footsteps that also cross the floor from time to time.

There's one little ghost with a big impact at the yacht club: a child named Jacob, who died in 1920 when he fell down the staircase. These days, it's said he hangs out at the top of those deadly stairs, peering out from the third level. Not everyone can see him there—but he's willing to appear for children when they stop by to say hello.

Unfortunately, in October 1938, things took a sad turn at Walbridge Park, too. Grounds crews were preparing for a parade, raking fall leaves into piles near the picnic area to clear the parade route. Then, they burned the piles to dispose of them. It was a relatively normal practice—but maybe not the best idea on a windy day... near a wooden roller coaster... and acres of other wooden rides!

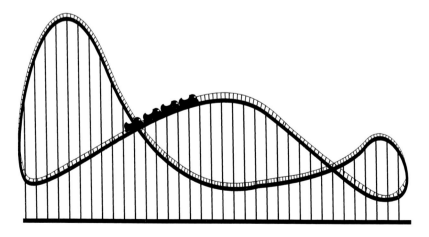

The wind must have carried a hot ember to the old coaster because it was up in flames before anyone knew what was happening. Worse still, the fire was spreading quickly. One by one, the wooden rides caught fire. Before anyone could stop the damage, almost all of the rides were destroyed. Only the merry-go-round remained. Parts of the amusement park were rebuilt, but it never regained its former splendor.

However, all was not lost. Remember when the newly formed Walbridge Park Zoo consisted of a single woodchuck? Well, there was much more than one woodchuck by 1939. In that year, the newly renamed "Toledo Zoo" had the second-largest collection of animal exhibits in the United States, behind only the Bronx Zoo in New York. Among attractions in Walbridge Park, Toledo Zoo was now center stage.

Today, Toledo Zoo is one of the city's top attractions and a hub of wildlife research and conservation. It's also a great place for animal lovers to work! It might not surprise you that those employees hear plenty of strange noises at the zoo. After all, today it's home to over 16,000 animals and about 700 species—everything from alpacas to zebra sharks. But those in the know at Toledo Zoo say it's not the

animals that make it one of the city's haunted hot spots.

Perhaps the spookiest spot of all is the Museum of Natural History. A renovation to the structure might have stirred up the spirits there. Or it might have just made them stand out more—because while the living employees changed their habits when the floor plan changed, the ghosts did not!

Wanda Davis recalls, "I saw a black figure of a man just floating in the hall where the Great Hall used to be. At first, I wasn't sure what I saw, but it happened two other times!"

Davis has also heard people talking late at night when she was the only one there—including one time that sounded like a man and a woman on a date, laughing and talking. Other staffers have heard doors slamming, seen lights flipping on and off in empty rooms, or felt a strong sensation of being watched.

Ghostly presences have also been felt in the animal buildings—perhaps the shadows of a few unlucky people who died at the zoo. In the early 1900s, two zookeepers were killed by animals: one was stabbed by an elephant's tusk, and the other was attacked by two zebras. In 1972, a man got the idea to climb into the polar bear enclosure and walk into the moat to approach the bears. It's unclear if he thought he would make friends with the polar bears or beat them in a wrestling match, but needless

to say, neither one of those things happened. When his body was pulled out of the moat later that day, the zoo director described it as "pretty eaten up."

Are all the zoo ghosts indoors? Possibly, but it seems they also like to haunt the houses nearby. Neighbors have reported cabinet doors moving by themselves, just like the doors in the Museum of Natural History. Others have heard footsteps in their attics. Shavaun Andrews recalled, "One night, the footsteps came down the steps, and my bedroom door flung open."

Talk about creepy!

One ghost, at least, seemed to be trying to make a friend. Holly Clark Burgete was four years old when she was chatting with a blond-haired little girl wearing a blue dress—or so she thought. Holly's mother observed the interaction and was so freaked out, the family sold the house and moved away.

Have you ever felt a strange presence at the zoo? Heard the slamming of a door or spotted something floating in the Museum of Natural History? If you do, it doesn't sound like there's anything to worry about. Just keep your distance from those polar bears.

Haunted Restaurants & Bars

It's not unusual for shadow people to become associated with restaurants and bars. These businesses tend to have lots of people on site as potential witnesses, including employees who make regular trips to the attics and basements where spirits love to lurk. They tend to have more renovations than other types of buildings, which stirs up any possible paranormal activity. And their security systems sometimes catch strange evidence we might otherwise miss. Toledo has no shortage of spirited eateries where you can grab a bite—and maybe also a fright!

Spaghetti Warehouse

The first recorded business at this address wasn't a restaurant but a lumber yard. The existing building went up as a beer-bottling plant in 1897, changing hands another couple of times before becoming Spaghetti Warehouse Italian Restaurant in 1976. It had taken a while for 42 South Superior Street to become the restaurant we know and love today, with pasta dinners on the menu and its signature full-size trolley in the middle of the dining room. But

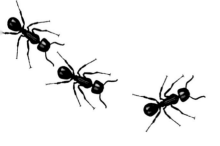

it didn't take long for two old spirits to make themselves known to the new owners!

Employees began noticing that something was going on when they'd set things down in one place and find them somewhere else entirely. A server might spend time carefully arranging the dining room with plates, silverware, and glasses on every table and chairs tucked in just-so—then return to find everything rearranged. One employee remembers cleaning up thoroughly after her Sunday night shift only to arrive Monday to find a mess.

"Chairs were everywhere, and sugar packets covered the floor," she recalled.

Some people have felt hidden hands

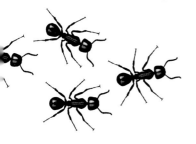

tapping their shoulders or pulling their hair. Others have sensed someone watching them when no one was there or heard whispers from empty spaces.

On the main floor, people think these whispers might belong to a woman who once worked for the bottling company and died in a tragic accident. Ghost hunter Al Luna says the woman's name is Sally, and she was born in the 1800s. Could that be the woman's voice one employee hears near the trolley when the restaurant is empty?

Another employee, a security guard, thinks he spotted Sally one night after closing. While walking into the dining room from the kitchen, he saw the trolley, as usual, in the middle of the empty dining room. Only the dining room wasn't empty: Through the trolley windows he thought he saw a figure sitting at the front of the restaurant. He walked around the trolley to get a better look. Whoever it was, they'd have to go because the restaurant was closed for the night. When he got within clear view, he was shocked to see a woman in an old-fashioned dress who looked like she was from another

time. She turned her head to look right back at him and then disappeared into thin air.

Luna says there is also a man on the premises, though no one can figure out much about him. All the employees know is that he likes to hang out in the basement, and they try to go there as little as possible. With bathrooms, storage spaces, and a game room down there, though, staffers and guests alike have been known to encounter this fearsome fellow from time to time.

Children are thought to be more sensitive to spirits, which might explain why one woman was mystified by how her grandson behaved in the restaurant's game room. He kept staring at

the back of the basement room, running toward it and then back to the game area. When it was time to go, the boy called out cheerfully, "Bye, Tony!" A bartender reports one spine-tingling trip to the storage room when she felt breath on the back of her neck. Multiple women have reported seeing a man appear before them while taking trips to the downstairs bathroom. That was weird enough—but two of them saw him walk right through a wall! Another was in the bathroom alone when she heard a stall door open and a voice call out her name.

The second floor and attic are said to be just as haunted. Chairs move on their own, voices come from nowhere, and a basket has floated in midair before settling eerily down again. One employee went to the attic to get something out of storage, and while she was looking for it, she heard a bodiless voice call out her name from the darkness!

Firefly

Like Spaghetti Warehouse, Firefly had a lot of lives before it became a restaurant. Originally, a house was on this site, but it burned down in 1873. Then the current structure was built to house a drugstore, then offices, an art studio, Firefly Lounge, and finally, under its newest owner, Firefly.

These days, the building is home to a fun nightlife scene... and a pretty funny ghost. After a 2021 renovation, Jenna and Alexa—two employees of what was then Firefly Lounge—were in the basement gathering supplies when they were startled by the sounds of a male voice in the room.

"Hello, darling," said the voice.

Jenna called back, "Who else is behind us?"

Without missing a beat, the voice answered, "It's just us."

That was all they needed to hear! The girls bolted upstairs as fast as their legs could carry them.

Tony Packo's

The original Tony Packo's set up shop down the road from the current location in 1902. Their sandwiches and ice cream sold in decent numbers... but their Hungarian sausages were a neighborhood sensation! Word spread, crowds followed, and Tony Packo's moved to the bigger space at 1902 Front Street and became a Toledo hot dog institution. You may have heard of their signature décor: celebrity-signed hot dog buns lining the walls! The place was quirky, the food was delicious, and people just couldn't seem to stay away. Even people who should have been long gone.

Ghost Hunter Chris Bores and his friend, Marie, a medium who communicates with spirits, visited the site to see what they could discover. Marie felt a strong presence of a male spirit who had been stabbed to death in the building. She said he was excited she could understand him and was begging her to tell his story! The ghost of a little girl had been spotted playing in the basement. Could she be related to his story?

Maybe she had been the one causing glass objects to crash to the floor in the gift shop or the sound of footsteps when no one was there. People observed other eerie signs, too. A flash of a figure who would appear . . . and then suddenly vanish. The creepy feeling that someone is standing right behind you. . . .

Chris learned of another violent death that might be tied to at least some of the building's unsettled energy. Long ago, there was a sheet metal business in the downstairs space, and the owner of the business lived in an apartment upstairs. One terrible night, the owner came home and got into a brutal fight with his wife and her brother. The enraged husband beat his wife, and the brother shot the husband, killing him. Police investigated the incident and declared the shooting self-defense, and that was the end of the story. Unless maybe those three still aren't quite finished with their fight.

Mancy's Steakhouse

Young Gus Mancy had very recently arrived in Toledo from Greece when he opened Mancy's Ideal Restaurant and Olde Tyme Saloon in this location just over a century ago. He started small—just one of four businesses in the building—but he worked hard, and the business grew quickly. People loved Gus's food, and the business was a quick success. Fifty years later, Gus bought the entire business and started renovations, looking forward to a proud new chapter. But then disaster struck: fire broke out in the building, and with the sprinkler systems shut down for the renovations, it soon grew out of control. The building was destroyed.

It took a lot of work and money, but the structure was rebuilt, and the restaurant reopened. Gus Mancy's restaurant carried on. In 2021, Mancy's Steakhouse celebrated one hundred years of service, looking splendid with family portraits on the wall—Gus himself front and center. It's really a milestone to be proud of... and it seems no one wants to be left out of the celebration.

There was a series of ghostly occurrences that made staff members feel they weren't alone at the restaurant, even when they were, well, alone. For instance, a server felt an unseen hand; others heard soft whispers coming from empty dining booths. People felt like they were being watched or followed but couldn't explain exactly why.

When ghost hunter Chris Bores and spiritual medium Marie went to Mancy's Steakhouse, they hoped to get some answers about who was behind the hauntings. Chris did some research about the 1970s fire and the restaurant's history. As for Marie, her gift would come into play when she walked into the restaurant and tried to receive energy from spiritual beings there. And she did—right away.

"It's of an old man," Marie said. Then she looked up at the first portrait on the wall: Gus Mancy. "That's him!"

Marie said there was a happy energy in the space. It seemed Gus and possibly other members of the family were there looking on with pride, aware that it was a big anniversary and happy to see the family doing well. Happy anniversary, Gus.

Georgjz419

When George Thompson was looking for a place for his next project, he was drawn to the old nineteenth-century building at 1205 Adams Street. He liked the tan brick structure with its distinctive row of porthole windows, especially because it was on a busy row of businesses that felt warm and welcoming to all Toledoans. He could envision the great nightclub it could become. But first, it would need some updates. So, George got to work gutting the building for renovation, and he soon found out the place was even more welcoming than he'd realized.

"I was working in the restroom," George recalls, "and I heard a plywood board slam down. I thought someone was in here. I yelled, 'I know someone is in here! I already called the cops!'"

George was only bluffing. He hadn't really called the police. Not only that, when he took a look around, he realized there *wasn't* anyone in there. He probably could have explained away the fallen board, but as construction continued, things got really strange—*spooky* strange. Tools started disappearing from one

place and reappearing in another, random place. Sounds he couldn't explain—some that sounded like voices—seemed to come out of nowhere.

By the time the club opened, George was pretty sure his new building had come with a resident ghost. It seemed, at least, that he was a kind of playful ghost. On a string of Christmas lights over the bar, George noticed one light swaying all by itself. A security camera caught a toy truck rolling across the basement floor, then vanishing before anyone

could investigate. Employees reported shadow figures and footsteps in the kitchen, and even stones being tossed across the bar at night!

A couple of years into operation, the ghost seemed ready to reveal his identity—and it put on quite a show to make the announcement. Security video caught the whole thing. First, the overhead lights turned off for no reason. Then, one light began rapidly blinking as if in Morse code—the long and short signals sometimes used by the military to transmit messages by radio. Next, another light next to the first started blinking, too. The video clip including the code-like blinking went on for fifteen minutes! George called in an expert to help figure out what on Earth was going on. Ghost hunter Chris Tillman arrived with a special radio device to help decipher the signal.

"Cooper... Cooper..." read the device. What did it mean?

They dug into the building's history and all the pieces started to fall into place. Orville Cooper, a World War II veteran, rented an upstairs room in the building in the 1970s. He died in 1978, but it seems he might have stuck around like a ghostly permanent resident.

As one memorable incident proved, he was something of a guardian angel, too. One night after closing, George set the building alarm, locked the doors, and headed out. Right after he left, the alarm went off as though someone had broken through the lock. George went back into the bar, reassured himself that no doors had been broken into, reset the alarm, and left again. Then, for a second time, the alarm went off with no apparent cause, and George went back into the bar to reset it. Was Orville up to something? The pattern kept repeating until George noticed an intruder hiding in the back room in the dark, waiting to be alone so he could rob the place. The alarm wouldn't have caught the intruder because technically he didn't break in. Orville caught him, though.

CHAPTER 6

A Book Break

There's something special about browsing the bookshelves of a public library. At these amazing institutions, you can find everything from fairy tales to travel guides, from mysteries to manga, from video games to...ghost librarians? There's something *extra* special waiting at these branches of the Toledo Lucas County Public Library. So, keep your eyes and ears open, and don't forget your library card! You never know what you might find.

Downtown Branch

If you're looking for stories with lots of action, you might want to browse the shelves on the second floor of the library's main branch. The librarians can help you choose a great read, and the ghosts might add a little drama of their own. An "old lady ghost" is said to have been lurking there for fifty years or more. She has been spotted by library patrons, young and old. Security guards, too, report seeing a human-like shadow appear mysteriously on their video feeds at night.

While on the second floor, many people have also reported hearing footsteps from above, even though nobody was up there. Who could be making those ghostly sounds? It's not clear, but if Toledoans from old times are trying to make their stories known, that might be where they'd go: the third floor is home to the library's local history collections and obituaries.

West Toledo Branch

We know that spirits sometimes stay with the building they died in, but does that go for *pieces* of the building they died in? That's how some people explain the ghost of a priest spotted by librarians working late at the West Toledo branch of the public library. Pieces of an old church were reused in its construction, and the priest's spirit might have come along for the ride!

Spiritual medium Marie felt another presence in the library. "This is a librarian from the old days. She loved kids and organizing the library events here.... She wants people to know she's still here, and she loves the kids. She wants them to come by whenever they can."

Birmingham Branch

Catharine Gorman was the dedicated first employee of the Birmingham branch of the library in 1925. She died in 1958, but that hasn't stopped her from going to work! Most people think Catharine is behind the haunted hijinks at this neighborhood library. Librarian Julie McCann recalls one especially memorable exhibit of dolls displayed in a locked glass case. Julie had the only key and made sure everything inside was secure. One morning when she arrived at work, however, Julie found one of the dolls turned completely around!

Other signs seem a little less like Catharine, such as loud knocks and the sound of a man clearing his throat. Then again, you can't judge a book by its cover.

Spooky Schools

Well-meaning adults sometimes encourage kids to get a good education by stressing the importance of staying in school. At these Toledo institutions, some people seem to have taken that idea to a whole other level!

University of Toledo

"UToledo," as it is lovingly known, is home to thousands of students who study in the libraries, crowd the sidelines to cheer on Rockets sports teams, and occasionally encounter some pretty creepy dorm mates.

One former student says, "One of the first-floor men's bathrooms has a ghost that turns water on in the showers. I turned it off, but then it turned it right back on!"

In classrooms, lights have been known to flick on and off during lectures. Even creepier, sometimes they just get dimmer as the teacher speaks. Is this the spirits' way of raising their hands to ask a question during class?

Some arts-loving ghosts are less interactive: Students report a feeling of being watched while in music classes on the top floor of University Hall and in a photography darkroom late at night. But more athletic ghosts like to keep active. Late one night in the field house, two students actually spotted a shadow figure practicing basketball!

Start High School

Like a great work of art, sometime hauntings reveal themselves bit by bit before you get the full emotional impact. That was the case for one art teacher at Start High School, who started noticing that the tools and supplies she'd place in one place would disappear and reappear somewhere completely different.

That continued for months, along with strange noises from the supply room that would stop as she approached. She might have felt curious, a little spooked, but not too frightened. That is until one night, when she was working late in the art room and happened to glance at a mirror on the wall. She saw her own reflection, and behind it, the reflection of a shadow person standing right beside her. The art teacher spun around to see who was there, but she was alone! Other teachers have witnessed similar shadows and noises in the room, but they can't agree who could be behind the haunting.

Reach Academy

Teachers and students at Reach Academy aren't sure what—or who—is behind the hauntings in the 1930s school building once known as St. Stephen's School. However, one ghostly presence in a main floor bathroom has become so familiar, they've decided to call her "Rosie."

"Rosie likes to hang around the bathroom area and turn on sink faucets and shut bathroom stall doors a lot," says one teacher.

Some think Rosie might be a former student. Others think she might be one of the nuns who taught at St. Stephen's. It seems many have decided to embrace Rosie's presence and go about their business. But not everyone feels so comfortable with this paranormal peeper, as a former teacher explained:

"I didn't enjoy working there late at night because I would go to the bathroom and feel like I was being watched the whole time. I would also hear odd sounds I couldn't explain."

Imagine if you couldn't even go to the bathroom without worrying that nuns or little girls might peer in! You might be cool with a haunted building... and still wish for a little less potty time with nosy Rosie.

Historic Downtown

Downtown Toledo sits right beside the Maumee River. It's a busy hub for the Glass City's business, sports, and historical life. It's also a center for some supernatural citizens who love calling the city center home—and don't want to stop any time soon.

Commodore Perry Hotel

Designs for this iconic 1927 Toledo building called for three towers rising above the main structure (only two of them were built in the final design), so that each of the 500 guest rooms had access to natural light. That's just the kind of thoughtful luxury that went into every detail of the Commodore Perry Hotel—from the first-floor lobby, restaurant, and ballroom to the bedrooms on the nineteenth floor, the Commodore Perry catered to guests' every need. It had every convenience imaginable including a telegraph office, bakeshop, personal dining rooms, and even a hospital, all on the second floor.

With its ideal location downtown and a reputation

for luxury, in its heyday the Commodore Perry Hotel attracted presidents, actors, and celebrities of every kind—including "the king" himself, Elvis Presley! After years of success, however, business slowed and the hotel closed its doors in 1980.

The next chapter for the historic hotel began in 1997, when the building underwent a huge renovation and then reopened as the Commodore Perry Apartments. Right away, the tenants started to notice some odd goings-on at the old "CP." A young girl appears on the first floor—sometimes playing in the ballroom, other times crying on the front steps. She has also been seen on the second floor, though since that space is now closed to the public, there are fewer reports of her there.

Heading upstairs, you just might encounter an elevator operator from beyond. Janet Amid reported being on an elevator that refused to let her select the floor she wanted. No matter how many times she pressed the button, it wouldn't light up. Maybe it's because someone else wanted to run the show. One person got onto the elevator and found a lady elevator operator on board. When the person got off the elevator, she turned back to look, and the elevator was empty!

If you manage to get up to the fourteenth floor, beware: residents say it's extra haunted. Mario, a tenant on the fourteenth floor, found

that every time he tried to go to sleep, a chill fell over the room, and a shadowy figure loomed over the bed. Understandably, Mario decided to sleep in the living room after that! It turns out someone died in his sleep in that apartment a decade before; the body remained there for days before it was removed. His spirit seems to have stayed behind, though, creating a haunting so strong it may even impact the neighboring apartment. Inside, the lights flicker on and off in a way no electrician can explain.

Hillcrest Arms Hotel

If having a dead body associated with your building means a ghost might haunt the premises, then you can imagine what might happen if you build on the site of a cemetery! That's the case at the Hillcrest Arms, which, like the Commodore Perry, is a former luxury hotel reinvented as a hip downtown apartment building.

One couple said they heard loud noises coming from the kitchen when they were in another room and saw black shadows lurking around the apartment. Another couple reported similar black shadows in their apartment, and they heard weird noises as well as creepy voices coming from nowhere. But perhaps the spookiest report comes from Scott Sifuentes, who recalls how scary it was to try to sleep at his friend's Hillcrest apartment.

"It would feel like someone was breathing by your ear. When you woke up, it would look like a shadow was walking into the bathroom. It was creepy!"

So, why in the world would anyone build a hotel on top of a cemetery? Well they *didn't*, exactly. Toledo's earliest settlers were buried in a couple of different locations: Forest Cemetery on the east side and Madison Cemetery on the west side. As the city grew and city planners laid out the streets that we know today, the new grid erased an old

thoroughfare called Territorial Road—and the cemetery that ran along it. The graves were moved to a different location, and as far as we know, every precaution was taken to relocate

them with dignity and care. But some of those early settlers might not have been happy about moving. Or maybe when the new Hillcrest Arms rose above their former resting place, they liked the look of it and decided to move right in!

CHAPTER 9

Repertoire Theatre

You can catch great live theater at this local treasure, which features plays with casts of all ages, for all ages—and even a couple of ghosts! Like many people who spend time in the theater, they've got lots of personality—and know how to add a bit of drama to the day!

George

The well-dressed man in the back of the theater enjoys watching shows take shape onstage. The tech crew and set designers have spotted him late at night sitting in the empty theater seats, watching the stage. He doesn't stick to the same seat every single time, but he does seem to have favorite parts of the theater—the left side and the center aisle. He's even been seen in the lobby. The crew got so used to seeing him, they named him "George." And they never give him too much trouble about not paying for a ticket to whatever show he thinks he's watching.

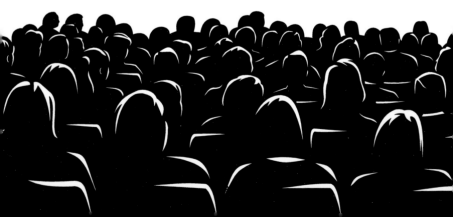

BETH HESTER is originally from the haunted city of New Orleans, where she sometimes heard ghostly footsteps in the very old house where she grew up... and awoke one morning to find a mysterious footprint on her ceiling! These days, she lives in New England with her husband, two children, and one spooky dog, and (most of) the footprints stay on the floor. You can find her at bethhester.com.

Check out some of the other *Spooky America* titles available now!

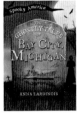   

Spooky America was adapted from the creeptastic *Haunted America* series for adults. *Haunted America* explores historical haunts in cities and regions across America. Here's more from the original *Haunted Toledo* author, Chris Bores.

A Ghostly Goodbye

We hope you've enjoyed your tour around Toledo's creepiest corners. You might have learned there are spots you'd like to avoid, but hopefully, you also learned that a lot of our spirits are sticking around because they're proud of their homes in Toledo. So, if you hear doors opening and closing when no one is around, or smell old-fashioned perfume in the air, or notice that the thing you left over *here* has suddenly reappeared over *there*, don't panic! It's probably just one of those Glass City ghosts having a little fun in the city they love.

from the cemetery shortly afterward, scratched up just like the boys.

Homes around the cemetery have had strange hauntings, too—like doors opening and closing on their own, strange noises, and, of course, those little girls coming out to play. Maybe all the paranormal activity in the graveyard has stirred up other ghosts nearby? Or maybe spirits willing to wander beyond the grave might be willing to wander even farther.

"My friends were in the cemetery at midnight, and there was a blue orb floating around, like, twelve feet in the air!" said one witness.

These witnesses left their encounters feeling freaked out—but mostly curious and amazed. Other visitors to Woodlawn have been less lucky. In one story from the 1950s, two teenagers were walking home through the cemetery late at night. One area was particularly foggy, and as they walked into the fog, they felt themselves being scratched violently! They got to the exit gate as fast as they could, and only then did the painful scratching stop. The boys told their parents what had happened. The parents called the police, and the police went into the cemetery to investigate. But no badge was going to deter these mean spirits. The police officers emerged

together, and in another, a little girl alone by a pond. Could these ghosts go together?

Other people have seen spooky signs that appear in energy form.

for her lost daughter. Interestingly, other people have spotted the ghosts of little girls in old-fashioned clothes playing in nearby neighborhoods—in one case, two girls playing

Woodlawn Cemetery

Our last stop is everyone's last stop: the cemetery. Woodlawn Cemetery is, of course, the final resting place of many, many people who have passed away. It seems not all of them, however, are all that ready to be restful.

Near the cemetery gates, the ghostly figure of a woman in a long white dress has been spotted wandering around, calling out

The Lady in White

The Lady in White appears in the upstairs office, though some people say they also spot her in the parking lot when they look out the office window. Besides appearing consistently to witnesses as a visible spirit, the Lady has another signature habit. When people leave the office late at night, she reminds them, "Turn off the lights, please!"